How to Invest in a Mobile Home Park for Business, Money and Profit

By

Dave Rousher

How to Invest in a Mobile Home Park – For Business, Money and Profit - 2015 by Dave Rousher Revised and update 2017

All rights reserved. No part of this book may be reproduced in any form without permission in writing from the author. Reviewers may quote brief passages in reviews.

Disclaimer and FTC Notice

No part of this publication may be reproduced or transmitted in any form or by any means, mechanical or electronic, including photocopying or recording, or by and information storage and retrieval system, or transmitted by email without permission in writing from the publisher.

While all attempts have been made to verify the information provided in this publication, neither the author nor the publisher assumes any responsibility for errors, omissions, or contrary interpretations of the subject matter herein.

This book is for entertainment purposes only. The views expressed are those of the author alone, and should not be taken as expert instruction or commands. The reader is responsible for his or her own actions.

Adherence to all applicable law and regulations, including international, federal, state, and local governing professional licensing, business practices, advertising, and all other aspects of doing business in the US, Canada, or any other jurisdiction is the sole responsibility of the purchaser or reader.

Neither the author nor the publisher assumes any responsibility or liability whatsoever on the behalf of the purchaser or reader of these materials. Any perceived slight of any individual or organization is purely unintentional.

This book has been professionally edited. If you find any errors please email the author at: http://drousher@amorgininvestmentgroupllc.com.

No links in this book, except those to Amorgin Investment Group, are affiliate links.

If you're trying to create a company, it's like baking a cake. You have to have all the ingredients in the right proportion. Elan Musk

HOW TO INVEST IN A MOBILE HOMEPARK

TABLE OF CONTENTS

Chapter 1 - Mobile Home Park Investing – An Overlooked Specialty Market

Chapter 2 – Mobile Home Parks vs. Apartment Buildings – The "Ins" and "outs"

Chapter 3 – Senior vs. Family Parks – The Final Showdown

Chapter 4 – Mobile Home Park Rating System – Find the Truth in the Stars

Chapter 5 - How to Price a Property – CAP Rates

Chapter 6 - Why Not Just Build a Mobile Home Park? Or Reinvent the Wheel While You Are At It?

Chapter 7 - Where Do I Begin? I Feel So All Alone

Chapter 8 - Where to Find the Best Mobile Home Park for You – So Many Things to Consider

Chapter 9 - Found the Park of My Dreams – What to Do Next?

Chapter 10 - What to Run From. Danger! Danger! Will Robinson!

Chapter 11 - How to Make Money – or Think like Daddy Warbucks

Chapter 1

MOBILE HOME PARK INVESTING

An Overlooked Specialty Market

I've been in the mobile home park real estate investment business for over 35 years. Despite my respect for the *Rich Dad, Poor Dad* books by Robert Kyosaki, I have never developed an interest in the rental housing industry. Apartment complexes with their "ins" and "outs" tenancy has always left me cold, and commercial strip malls are not my cup of tea.

"So why" you ask "are you in the mobile home park industry?"

Simple, my father-in-law (who gave me my first position as a real estate agent), Donald H. Barnett, had been in the mobile home park (MHP) business since the days when they were called Gypsy Camps (which got their start in the 1940s). He had carved out a good career selling "trailer parks" as they were called at the time, and I liked the concept.

To my knowledge, he was the first person to write a book about investing in the mobile home park business. His 1974 best seller "Let's Talk Mobile Home Parks" was a short and sweet paperback that offered lots of helpful ideas for anyone interested in trying out a new, and then, up and coming industry and several banks used it as a source for lending on parks.

It has been over 40 years since Don wrote his book. It has been 50 years since he staked his claim by taking a chance on this often overlooked specialty real estate market. I am proud to say that our industry has grown, and it has proven itself to be a viable model for real estate investors who aren't afraid of rolling up their sleeves and getting into the trenches.

In 1978, when I joined the family business, mobile home park investing had just started to catch on. A few savvy investors had started testing the waters by building new communities that catered to senior and family living needs. Others chose to purchase existing properties and upgrade them. Today there are approximately 50,000 MHPs across the country.

The demand for MHP spaces continues to rise as individuals become dissatisfied with renting from apartment complexes. Many Baby Boomers are making the decision to move into MHPs as they sell the big homes they raised their families in so they can travel, or spend more time at the golf course.

Affordable housing is moving out of reach of so many people now days - owning a mobile home is a reasonably priced way for low income, downsizing seniors, or first time home buyers, to become part of the American Dream – that of being a home owner. By renting a space in a local MHP, they can enjoy the pride and peace of having their own place, the freedom to have a bit of land to plant a yard or garden in, while enjoying the benefits of community living.

As a mobile home park investor, you will be joining a small group of confident folks who have gained experience in a field that not many have taken a chance in. It wasn't until Warren Buffet purchased Clayton Homes, Inc. for $1.7 billion in 2003 that people started to take notice of this small, specialized industry. Buffet's company,

Berkshire Hathaway, already knew what you are going to be learning from this book.

With the right research, proper due diligence and sound business practices, MHPs are generally recession proof, give great cash flow, offer good tax deductions and provide significant value in the area of appreciation.

Ok, I see that you are still reading so I think it is safe to guess that you are not one of those people who have stayed away from MHP investing because you are afraid of the label "trailer trash." You won't be surprised to learn that Wikipedia has a definition for "trailer trash" which is:

__Trailer trash__ (or trailer park trash) is a derogatory North American English term for a small percentage of poor people living in a trailer or a mobile home. It is particularly used to denigrate white people living in such circumstances and can be considered to fall within the category of racial slurs.

It is this classification that led to the industry-wide name change from trailer park, to mobile home

Park, and now manufactured home community or land lease communities.

Let me be completely honest, there are still quite a few trailer parks that live up to the "trash" name - more than any of us in the industry would like to admit to. These parks give the rest of us a bad reputation. The owners refuse to do anything by way of upgrading their property because they just don't care. They take in rents, and give nothing in return.

These owners soon have a trailer park full of low income tenants, and tenants who take no pride in their homes or in their neighborhoods. These parks, and tenants, and owners, are in reality true *trailer trash*. They earned the name fair and square and no amount of fancy talk will change the truth of things.

Despite the few poorly maintained, unattractive MHPs that exist today, the manufactured housing sector has come a long way from its roots in the flimsy 2" X 2" walled, aluminum wired, 10' X 50' and 12' X 60' mobile trailers that were being built in the early 1950s and 1960s.

On June 15, 1976, the U.S Department of Housing and Urban Development was created. Stringent laws were implemented. Manufactured housing became regulated. The shoddy unsafe housing hammered out and sold to unsuspecting home buyers of the past, was stopped.

Today's home buyers will find that manufactured homes are built to the same standards as stick built housing (UBC Code), and are often indistinguishable from them. A mobile home buyer can even order porches and garages. Some homes offer high end amenities such as working fireplaces, whirlpool tubs, hardwood cabinets and flooring and/or stainless steel appliances. Just as today's manufactured homes are nothing like they were "back in the day," modern manufactured home communities offer such upscale amenities as playgrounds, walking paths, community parks, club houses, pools, Jacuzzis, tennis courts and even golf courses. Many of the newer modern MHPs can compete with, and surpass, upscale apartment complexes and condos.

One aspect of the manufactured housing market that has not changed is its affordability.

Depending on what part of the country one lives in, the costs of building a stick built home range from 20% to 65% more than a manufactured home; this excludes the cost of land and putting in utilities.

Although some of the fancier manufactured homes can sell in excess of $100,000, most are sold from between $35,000 to $65,000. Contrary to popular belief, the newly built manufactured homes do appreciate in value, just like stick built homes, depending upon the market in their area.

A mobile home is the least expensive form of detached housing. Stick built houses are priced at somewhere between $115.00 and $250.00 up per square foot (depending on location), while a mobile home can cost between $35.00 and $55.00 per square foot.

As previously stated, mobile homes are regulated by the Department of Housing and Urban Development. Regulated for consistent quality at an affordable price, mobile homes are a good value in today's home ownership market. As a home owner, a purchaser of a mobile home has the same perks as a person with a stick built home. They can take the interest payment they make on their home payment as a tax deduction, and they can decorate the home as they please. Their home will reflect their individual personality and not that of a sterile apartment complex.

Apartments are often noisy because of common floors, ceilings, and walls. Frequently apartment complexes have no open play areas for families to enjoy, and generally pets are not allowed. This does not create a sense of community, or neighborhood.

MHP community tenants, who own their own homes, lease the underlying land from the park owner. Pad rents can range from $200 to $800 per month depending on location and the market dynamics (there is a park in Newport Beach, California where the lot rents are over $1500 per month and 10' X 50' rehabbed homes can sell upwards of $250,000). These rent fees generally include trash removal but not the other utilities - water, sewer, gas and electricity.

From an investment perspective, lenders/investors often view MHPs as hybrid properties, with the characteristics of both rental apartments and single family homes. Some MHP investors have chosen to own rental homes along with the land, to generate additional income.

Let me interject that from my experience if you are not a "hands on" type of investor, willing and able to handle rentals personally or have deep pockets to have someone do it for you, renting out mobile homes can end up being a nightmare. Admittedly, there is lots of money to be made from renting homes, but statistically tenants in rental homes only stay for between six and twelve months. If you are not prepared to roll up your shirt sleeves and fix any issues left by your retreating renter in a cost effective manner, rental homes can become expensive.

Over the years, I have found that a tenant who owns their own home generally stays for approximately five years. When the tenant/homeowner makes the decision to leave, they usually will sell their home to an outside purchaser, who will then become your tenant. This is because of the cost aspect to move a home.

With rental mobile homes, I have found that I have the same difficulties that apartment landlords face. Those issues being that tenants are highly mobile, and generally when they move out they leave *your* home in disrepair and *your* repair costs really eat in to the bottom line of *your* profit.

If you choose to have rental mobile homes, ask yourself the following questions:

- Who will do the rehab work and remove the trash that will be left behind?

- Will that be you, your manager, or will you be hiring an independent contractor?

Also, by adding rental homes to your MHP, you will be doubling the amount of work your on-site manager will have to handle (even if he/she isn't fixing up the vacated homes or cleaning up messes). Normally, an on-site manager will take care of community landscaping, community buildings (office, clubhouse etc.) and collect rent. With rentals, your manager will also become a paid babysitter to tenants who don't care about community, the park rules and regulations, or personal property.

Another issue that will arise is the fact that lenders will not treat the rental income as part of the park's valuation should you chooses to refinance or sell. They prefer to stick with the lot rent. Also, if your rentals are not well maintained a bank may not give you a loan at all. Let me add that normal lenders shy away from properties with large numbers of rental homes. To them, this is a big red flag that something is either wrong with the area economics, or the management.

A typical park manager will work at a community for five or six years. When rental homes are added to the mix, I have seen managers leave in less than eight months. Every time a manager moves on, you are left with the job of hiring and retraining your new employee. This is costly, time consuming, and a pain in the rear. Are you getting the idea that I think rental homes are a **headache**?!.

I have always told my employees and investors to "make your life easy." I don't see owning and managing rental homes as "easy." That being said, I've met some heartier, younger souls than I, who want nothing but rental homes in their parks because they adore the cash flow and find the extra work exciting and worth the effort. After all a lender or prospective buyer for your property would much rather see a full park with rental homes than a park that is say 70% occupied. Another excellent area of potential is to purchase properties with some vacancies. Many times vacancies are the direct result of mismanagement, or lack of interest on the part of the current owner. Many early MHPs were built and run by mom and pops. Many of these mom and pops are now in their 70s and 80s and are tired of taking care of the business they have owned and managed for decades.

To take advantage of a situation such as this, you as a knowledgeable buyer will be able to fill these vacant spaces with new homes, and tenants who are paying you space rent. Paid monthly space rents where vacancies once were not only adds value to your investment, but puts lots of extra cash in your pockets and will decrease some of your maintenance expenses (since you won't be taking care of the vacant space any longer).

Here is a very simple example:

Mr. and Mrs. John Jones built their MHP in the early '70s. They are now in their 80s and want to retire. Their children have no interest in taking over the business, so they want to sell. The downside is that they have not advertised space availability over the years as tenants moved their homes out. Vacant spaces have never been an issue to them because their property is completely paid for and the cash flow that they receive is more than enough for them to live on.

The park has 100 spaces, but 25 are currently vacant. The property is located in a good section of town, has large spaces, and other than needing homes on those empty lots, and some simple maintenance and repairs, is a good investment.

Let's say you purchase the park for $2,193,750 which represents an 8% CAP Rate (I explain CAP Rates later in this book). You get in there and clean up the park, advertise and bring in 25 homes to fill those vacant spaces. Not only will you have increased your cash flow by up to 50%, but the property could easily have appreciated 33% over say a three year period. (I have not included any of the math here, but if you would like further explanation on this – get in touch with me at: http://drousher@amorgininvestmentgroupllc.com and I'll gladly ship it off to you!

Which brings us to another area of money making potential - Rent Raises. Yep, by raising the rents on your newly acquired, now full, 100 space MHP by $10.00 per month, your rent income will increase $1,000 monthly, which equates to $12,000 more annually.

This uptick in cash flow will also raise your property value by approximately $150,000. With this increase in cash flow along with filling the 25 vacant spaces, you can sell your newly polished jewel for $3,022,500. Not a bad profit for a little work.

Since we are speaking of potential here, you may be thinking to yourself that once you raise the rents in the park, there will be a **potential** for tenants to move their **mobile** homes out and down the road to a less expensive location.

Mobile homes are not mobile anymore, and moving one is not as easy as it was 35 years ago. As manufacturing companies began to build better homes (because of new laws), they also began to build larger homes as well. Wherein in the '50s, '60s and '70s mobile homes actually had axles and wheels attached underneath that stayed with the home once it was set on a lot, those days are *long* gone.

The newer, better homes are sturdier and heavier than those in the past, and if a tenant thinks that they can hook their home up to a truck and haul it down the road they are sadly mistaken. Along with towing something the size of a 16' X 80' manufactured home being too large for a simple truck to haul, the likelihood of it being a street legal move without the proper permit is really remote.

"Well the tenant can hire a MH mover," you say. Yep, they sure can, but mobile home movers are not cheap. To tear down, move, set up and re-level, and depending on the distance the unit is to be hauled, can easily cost a customer $5,000 or more.

Let's be honest, most mobile home owners do not have that kind of money in their savings accounts. It isn't even cost effective to spend $5,000 to save

$10.00 or so in space rent per month. It would take 41.6 months to pay for the home to be moved to a new park, and what will the tenant do when the park owner in their new location raises the rent? As long as your rent raises are "reasonable" the likelihood of a tenant moving out is nil.

An unhappy tenant has the option to sell their home on its current space. This is a benefit to both homeowner and park owner. The homeowner will receive a larger profit from the sale of their home by having it already on a space in a park, while you the landlord will continue to have a rented pad with paying tenants.

I have given annual rent raises for the past 30 years in all of my parks, even if it is only for a dollar. Every year a few "For Sale" signs go up in front windows or out on lawns. Tenants march in to the manager's office and protest the rent raise, swear they won't pay and are moving out. The manager always understands because he/she isn't the one who raised the rents (it was *you*, the nasty landlord). The tenants aren't happy, but at least they are able to voice their opinions. It has been my experience that within two weeks, all of the "For Sale" signs will be removed.

Or, maybe you decide that the park you have is perfect for you, and your future goals don't involve the sale of your "baby". You love the location; it makes tons of money, is close to where you live and provides you lots of tax deductions. Now, with this decision, you have put yourself into another area of profit making potential. This is because one day after years of happy ownership, you will wake up and realize that your beloved MHP is now surrounded by high end housing and shopping centers.

Your accountant points out to you that the highest and best use of the land is not that of being a mobile home park. He shows you building plans of a hospital that can be built right where *your* park is. He also explains how you are going to make a LOT of money from the sale of this little gem.

Historically, the above scenario occurs to MHPs that were built between 40 and 60 years before the area became "the place to be." Building a park in, or very close to, town has always been the biggest cost factor when building a new park. For that reason, buying land out of town would have been the best business decision for the original builder. This kept costs down and the neighbors didn't complain because they were probably horses, chickens and other livestock. Actually, quite a few builders were the farmers themselves.

One thing to remember- 50 or 60 years ago people didn't expect clubhouses, playgrounds or even paved roads for that matter. In those days the tenant/owners wanted one thing - a place to put their home, an area where they could put up a fence, till a little garden and to have a dog or two.

Most mobile homes in those days didn't have laundry areas, so a laundry facility made of wood, brick or cinder blocks was added as an extra feature that could bring in income from washer/dryer use. The utilities generally ran underground and were made of clay pipe for the sewer, and galvanized pipe for the water system.

What you have now is an Oldie Goldie. Your accountant points out that the infrastructure is antiquated and if it hasn't had any problems yet, it will soon. Also, since it is a vintage facility, the laundry is probably no longer in use because people have their own machines in their homes these days. And let us think about those old homes – they are between 10' X 50' and maybe 12' X 60' homes. Today these single wide homes have evolved into 16' X 80' and the double wide homes are 36' X 80', your older spaces can't accommodate the larger units.

That brings up the question of vacancies in these old MHPs. If *your* MHP can only accommodate the 10' X 50' or 12' X60' units (and your park is not situated right on the ocean in Newport Beach, California), you will have a problem filling up spaces. You have two choices here:

> (1). Buy an old home that fits the space, completely rehab it and find someone willing to purchase it. However, you will probably lose money because the purchase and rehab costs will be more than what you can sell it for, or

> (2). You can order a new custom made home from the manufacturer that will fit in that small lot, have it delivered and set up,

and then sell the home for what you can get for it.

Your beloved cash cow is running out of milk. It is time for it to transform into something bigger and better – STEAK!

Yep, sell her now. What are land values in the area? I bet they are a lot higher than they were when you first invested, and you have had years of rental income flowing into your bank account. As your accountant is willing to point out - let the new buyer worry about the development potential, it is time for you to find a bigger, better, and younger park to buy, it's time to move on!

Recap – What MHP Investing Can Offer You

- Stable income – residents own their own homes – costs to move these homes are high, and communities to move them into are limited.
- People are always looking for affordable housing that is their own – not someone else's.
- Because MH tenants own their own homes they take better care of the property and

their investment, as opposed to someone who rents.
- MH tenants live in their homes for approximately five years. Renters average around six month's tenancy.
- Operating Costs - are lower than for other rental properties such as apartment buildings – MHP owners can hire fewer on-site staff because there are less property maintenance issues. These issues are limited to common areas, utility services, a small number of buildings, and to collecting rents.
- Resistant to Recession – Tenant/home owners are motivated to pay their space rent because they own the home.
- Stable Return –As spaces fill up and by implementing consistent rent raises, the cash flow grows.
- Appreciation – Effective management practices by an experienced professional, along with crucial upgrades, add value and appreciation to the property.

Chapter 2

MOBILE HOME PARKS vs. APARTMENT BUILDINGS

The "Ins" and "Outs"

I can't state this fact enough – every city in every state in the country will always need affordable housing. Condos, apartments or mobile home parks fill that ticket. However, mobile homes are the least expensive detached housing opportunity available today in the housing market.

In general, when given the chance to enjoy the benefits of home ownership and the tax advantages involved, people will purchase a home. Home owners tend to take care of their homes and the area surrounding it, while apartment renters generally just don't care how the dwelling looks because it isn't theirs.

Yes, mobile home owners might allow water to run down the sewer (if they aren't paying for it) during the winter so their pipes don't freeze, but

MH owners don't punch holes in their walls, trash their carpets or tear doors off of the hinges and steal appliances. Why would they do that to their investment?

Best of all, you the MHP owner, don't have to repair or replace that broken toilet or water line that always breaks at the worst possible time.

Once a MH is moved into a park the normal life span of that home is at least 35 years. That is 35 years of tenant/homeowners paying you rent. As the MHP owner you will not be the one cleaning up the interior and exterior of the property when a tenant moves out.

Have you ever heard of an apartment owner not having some downtime and expenses involved with tenant turnover? Every day/month that an apartment unit is vacant is lost revenue. Every penny put into fixing or replacing anything in an apartment is more money lost. With a MHP there is no time or money lost on these kinds of expenses because you do not own it!

Furthermore, it costs less to run a MHP than an apartment complex. A general rule of thumb with a MHP is a 30% to 40% expense factor, while with an apartment it is between 50% and 65%.

Along with having lower expenses, MHPs have higher depreciation factors to offset income on taxes. With an apartment building, the stick built portion is generally depreciated at 27.5 years for the structure itself. Since there are generally few to no buildings involved with a MHP, the depreciable aspects are the roads, water and sewer lines, electric poles etc. These are considered improvements/amenities and they are depreciable over a 15 year lifespan. This is a major tax benefit and in most cases you can use a 75% improvement to 25% land cost for the project!

As a MHP owner, when you raise the rents from $5.00 to $20.00, moving out of the park is not generally the first thing a tenant will do (I have already noted that moving a home to a new community is very expensive and not worth the hassle). However, when an apartment dweller receives a rent raise it isn't much of a hardship for them to pack their belongings and be gone (leaving you holding a bag full of cleaning and repair expenses in the process).

Recap – Why Mobile Home Parks are better than Apartments

- Home owners take care of their homes – apartment renters do not.
- MHP owner owns the land the home sits on – does not need to worry if tenant's toilets or water heaters need to be replaced because they don't own them.
- When a tenant sells their home, landlord still receives rent from a new client and doesn't have to do any repairs for damage to the home.
- MHPs experience a lower turnover rate than apartments – average tenancy in MH is five years compared to 6 to 12 months with an apartment.
- The longevity of a MH in a park is 35 years.
- Employee and general expenses are lower in a MHP.
- Tax depreciation is better with MHP because owner depreciates improvements which have a shorter life span (15 years).

- Raise the rents at a MHP and tenants can't move out as easily as an apartment dweller.

Chapter 3

SENIOR vs. FAMILY PARKS

The Final Showdown

Everyone knows that the state of Florida is senior citizen heaven. Florida has the most mobile home parks in the country. Florida's population growth has continued to rise annually by 1.36%, and is the fastest growth state in the country for senior citizens.

Entire MHP communities have been built around the senior citizen active lifestyle. Gated communities, pools, saunas Jacuzzis, tennis courts, clubhouses, social activities, even golf courses have been built to accommodate this client demographic.

Senior citizens can be the best tenants in the world. They pay on time and in general you don't have worries about bounced checks or non-payment of rent as often as you do with a family park. Also, seniors tend to keep their lots beautiful, care about their neighbors and their communities, and don't throw raging keggers.

On the downside, senior citizens are often limited to a set income and rent raises can play havoc on their ability to afford these raises. Due to this there are often laws which vary from state to state, that regulate how much an owner can raise rents in their parks. Rent control laws can keep a hardworking MHP owner from making a profit if taxes, water, sewer and other expenses go up, and these laws won't allow you to offset these costs. So, before you buy a senior park or any park for that matter, check state and local laws.

Another benefit of having senior tenants is that they tend to live in their homes for a longer period of time than families. Since they are retired for the most part, they are not looking for a better job that will require them to move.

However, we are all aware that seniors pass away. When a tenant passes, you will have a home that is not only vacant with lot rent that isn't being paid, but you will have to deal with the heirs. If there are no heirs you will need to work with the state, or a bank, with regard to the disposition of the home. Once that is taken care of, you will then have to fill the vacant space and find yourself another senior citizen tenant to occupy that home.

Families frequently come and go and Landlords often have problems with children fighting, and I've seen more tenant disputes occur over this subject than I care to remember. Younger tenants throw loud parties, are often late with rents, and are more apt to bounce checks, keep messy yards and break playground equipment (guess the seniors don't like to play on the swings and slides).

On the upside, you don't have to worry about complying with all the federal and state laws set forth with owning a senior community.

Recap – Senior vs. Family MHPs –

- Seniors are more stable in making rent payments.

- Seniors keep their spaces cleaner.

- Seniors don't throw keggers.

- Senior parks have laws regulating them and are often subject to Rent Control.

- Seniors live on fixed incomes.
- Seniors stay in their homes longer than families.
- Seniors often pass away leaving vacant homes or vacant spaces.

Chapter 4

MOBILE HOME PARK RATING SYSTEM

Find the Truth in the Stars

When I begin my personal MHP search, I have already done my research with regard to where I want to be located etc. but, there are other things I need to take into consideration as well. I look for mid-range properties or three star parks.

"What is a *star*?" you ask. Well, it is an old school system of rating parks that helps lenders and investors assess, differentiate, and place a value on MHPs. It was adapted from the Woodall's RV Park and Campground Directory star rating system. Since trailer parks received their genesis from camp grounds, it was a logical move for real estate brokers and agents to use this system when describing a property with trailers and mobile homes.

The Manufactured Housing Institute (http://www.manufacturedhousing.org), a national trade association, formalized and developed the five star rating systems that take various attributes into consideration. The higher the rating, the nicer the park will be. The higher the rating, the easier it will be to secure financing with attractive terms, and of course the higher the rating, the higher the price of the property.

Attributes that buyers and lenders use to create a star rating include whether the streets are paved or unpaved, ratio of singlewide or doublewide homes/lots, what amenities a park has, such as clubhouse, pool etc., overhead or underground utilities, occupancy, on-site management and the properties' general appearance.

Five-star communities along with having clubhouses and pools are often located in prime locations such as coastal retirement areas.

Generally, lower star properties are located in secondary and tertiary markets, have no doublewide homes and have gravel or poorly paved streets.

Condition of utilities and amenities are also taken into consideration.

As previously stated, I prefer medium to lower range properties, generally two to three star parks. I tend to stay away from one star parks because by and large, they are in bad communities, and have been allowed to fall to such a level that no amount of money will revitalize it, or the community.

I do like four star parks if I can get one for the right price and there is upside potential. It is the park amenities and adult vs. senior that make the difference between a four and five star community.

I prefer older properties. Insurance is less expensive because you won't be paying for pools, clubhouses etc. also if there is room to expand, there is always an opportunity for you, the buyer, to add the amenities if you want them to create value to your property. Adding value lowers the CAP Rate (see next chapter to learn about CAP Rates) at time of sale.

Another thing I look for along with good economics and growth are properties which are along or near water. Water adds value and a water location can't be duplicated.

Recap – What About the Stars?

- MHPs are rated using s*tars* – 1 being the lowest to 5 being the highest.

- The higher the star rating the more expensive the MHP will be.

- The higher the star rating the more amenities a MHP will have.

Chapter 5

HOW TO PRICE A PROPERTY

CAP Rates

Local market dynamics will affect the value of a manufactured housing community, as will the operating expenses, vacancies and property condition. CAP Rates are the best way to ascertain the value of a MHP.

CAP Rates take into consideration the real income and all of the expenses, including the expenses that the seller forgot to put on the Profit and Loss Statement that he gave you. What is interesting about CAP Rates is just the opposite of what you might think. The **lower** the **CAP Rate** the **higher** the **value** of the property and vice versa.

How does one figure out the CAP Rate?

First you take the income and subtract all of the expenses except the mortgage payment and depreciation - that figure is called the Net Operating Income (NOI).

You then divide that number by whatever CAP Rate might be appropriate for the type of park you are considering. So, let's say your Net Operating Income is $100,000 and this type of park affords a CAP Rate of 8%. You divide the NOI by 0.08% and that will give you a value of $1,250,000.

If you are given a price for a park and the NOI, and you want to figure out what the CAP Rate is, you will take the NOI and divide it by the Sales Price X 100.

So, if you have an NOI of $135,000 and a Sales Price of $1,600,000, you will divide $135,000 by $1,600,000 and that will give you a CAP Rate of 8.44%.

You can then compare the CAP Rate of the park you are considering with CAP Rates of similar properties that have sold in the area, and parks that are currently for sale, to see if your park is in line or not.

In general CAP Rates will range from the mid 5% to 10% for parks that are really worth going after.

CAP Rates can vary widely, even within a single market, often driven less by geographic location than by characteristics of an individual community and its potential buyers.

As of 2016 CAP Rates nationwide ranged from 5.75% to 10.5%. Large amenity rich properties that have public utilities and no rental homes are in the most demand, and therefore sell for lower (meaning at a higher price) CAP Rates.

Recap – CAP Rates –

- The local market will often dictate CAP Rates for properties in their area.

- The lower the CAP Rate, the higher the price of the property.

- To figure out a CAP Rate – Subtract expenses (except mortgage payment and depreciation) from property's real income to get Net Operating Income. Take the NOI and divide by the CAP Rate (could be anywhere from 5% to 15%).

- Compare CAP Rate of property you are considering by those in the area.

Chapter 6

WHY NOT JUST BUILD A MOBILE HOME PARK?

Or Reinvent the Wheel While You Are At It?

I can't count how many times people have approached me with the "great idea" of building a brand new mobile home park. Just the idea of having something new, shiny and in perfect condition from the day you begin business has appeal. However, the reality and costs involved in building a new community today are not easy to swallow.

It could be the "trailer trash" stigma rearing its ugly head again, but the fact of the matter is that not many new properties are being built anymore due to federal, state, county and city regulations.

To get a MHP off of the ground takes a lot of **time** and **money**. Plans need to be engineered and agreed to by the city fathers, all state and federal regulations must be complied with, the property needs to be acquired, and people need to be hired to build the infrastructure – pads, roads, water, sewer, other utilities and any buildings your heart desires (the least of which needs to be an office).

If you get past all of this (because your pockets are just overflowing with greenbacks), you will need to promote your new baby with advertising and maybe even purchase a few units to set up and show off as model homes.

 How will you get these model homes and have them transported and set up? Will you use cash, or finance them? Then you will need some kind of sales team to help you sell homes to prospective tenants. Once homes are purchased by new home buyers, the overseeing of the moving in of the homes and set ups needs to be considered. As of this writing the bigger players I know of who will put a mortgage on a mobile home are 21st Mortgage (https://www.21stmortgage.com) and Vanderbilt Homes (http://www.vmfhomeloan.com). I am sure there are other banks that will do this service, but these two are the heavyweights that I have used in the past.

Instead of hiring a sales team and purchasing some homes to use as models, maybe you would prefer to get a local dealership to bring in homes to sell. That way *they* will have to put in all of the time, work and money. Of course they would be reaping the sales profits. Make sure you personally oversee the screening of potential home purchasers, especially when using an outside sales team, to make sure new tenants are a good fit for your new project.

 I've had dealers sell homes at very low cost, to almost anyone who is breathing just to make their commission. No matter who sells your homes, protect yourself from bad tenants. Just having breath and life and a small down payment does not constitute good tenancy to me.

Then last but certainly not least, let me remind you that this entire process won't be completed overnight – it could take years to finish – that means years where money is going out, and very little if anything is coming back in.

The process often isn't pretty. I can tell you about this from hard experience, because long ago in my beloved state of Montana, my partner and I came up with the brilliant idea to build a high end mobile home community.

Our dream was to build a five star neighborhood. We had plans for a club house, pool, walking trails, plus a first rate playground. This was to be built on farmland with views across the road of a beautiful river. We were ecologically sensitive to the river's flow and made sure that no contamination would ever enter the waterway.

This facility wasn't going to be your "normal" mobile home community; homes were going to be brand new doublewides. To keep the streets free from extra cars, boats and RVs there was to be a fully fenced storage area that could include stick built storage units. The landscaping design was set up so that it would complement the natural plants in the area. Who wouldn't want something this upscale in their community? Also note that this was to be built five miles out of town where only wheat was growing and cows grazed!

With high expectations and the knowledge that we were bringing in a planned community that would be accepted by one and all, we brought our ideas before the county council. What a surprise the locals had for us! The room was filled to capacity with angry neighbors convinced that we were money hungry SOBs from California, intent on destroying their home town and the water corridor in particular.

The engineer who created the plans, along with my partner, was up in front of the room facing the angry mob and all of their put-downs. Safely in the back of the room I tried to make myself small and unnoticeable. A realtor friend standing next to me gave me a nudge in the side and whispered "Now you know how Custer felt."

Yeah, we were definitely massacred that evening. We weren't even able to present our vision, let alone have it brought to a vote. It wasn't easy being considered the devils of our community who should be expelled from town on a rail after being tarred and feathered. It hurt our egos, dreams, and pocket books to say the least.

Yet, ever a glutton for punishment, I admit that I would not turn down a new build opportunity given the right circumstances, in the right community, under the right conditions. There is a first time for everything and I do believe the MHP industry needs some new neighborhoods for the many folks looking for good affordable housing.

Recap – Why Not Build a New MHP?

- Federal, state, local laws must all be followed to the "T".

- Hiring engineers and contractors to build infrastructure is very expensive.

- It could take years to break even or make a profit.

- You might find out how Custer felt at the Battle of the Big Horn if your community does not agree that an MHP would be an asset.

Chapter 7

WHERE DO I BEGIN?

I Feel So Alone

Mobile home parks come in many shapes, sizes and property conditions. They are located everywhere in the United States and I'm quite sure you have seen lots of them in your lifetime already.

Since you are still reading this book I think it is safe to say that you are interested in moving ahead and becoming a MHP owner yourself. I expect that you asking "Where do I begin?"

To start with, I always suggest that potential buyers consider what their investment goals are. Ask yourself the following questions:

- What kind of return do you want to get on your money?

- What kind of property best meets your portfolio needs?

- Do you want a fixer upper, one that needs little or no changes, or something in between?

- How about location – do you envision your park being close to home, within a few hours' drive, or accessible by air?

- What are your investment goals? Obviously everyone's investment goals are different, but you need to ask yourself "why do I want this type of MHP?"

- Are you looking for the higher than average cash flows?

- Do you want the higher depreciation aspect of this type of investment to help offset some of your other taxable income?

- Are you in it for the long haul, and want long term appreciation that a manufactured home community can give you?

- What total return on your investment money do you want/need?

Obviously, there are pros and cons to consider when answering each of these questions. I will do my best to provide you with the tools to help in making your final investment decision. Ultimately, you need to have your goals well defined and keep them at the forefront of your mind when you are looking for a park to buy.

There are basically three types of communities that are available today.

> (1). The adult/senior community: The adult/senior community will fall generally within the 5-6% CAP Rate ranges and will afford cash flows in the area of 4-6%.

> (2). The family community: The basic family community will be in the 6.5-9% CAP Rates and the cash flows from these investments will be approximately 7-12%.

> (3). What I call the "cash machine" or the "don't eat before you go" type of property: they make a lot of cash flow but they are old, have many vacancies, may have rentals, need upgrading and require lots of time. The "don't eat before you go" parks have

CAP Rates of 10-15% and the cash flows upon the close of escrow can range from 12-20%.

Having a clear idea concerning CAP Rates and also having answered your personal investment questions listed above, you now have a good idea as to how much time and energy you want to devote to your project, and what the cash flow figure for your purchase should be. It is time to begin your search!

You know which type of property best meets your needs. Within these property types you will find that different time, money and management levels are required to create your MHP winner. Once again, consider the reality of the variations in parks.

- The Fixer Upper has the advantage of lots of upside potential for future rent raises and have the value add aspect. Fix all of the deferred maintenance, pave the roads, clean up the landscaping, rehab or move out abandoned homes, bring in new houses and new home owners, fix up or purchase nice rental homes, and watch the money flow in.

- A Five Star top of the line community with all the bells and whistles is probably everybody's dream. I know it was mine with that river front project. However, be prepared to pay TOP dollar for the investment and don't expect to get TOP dollar in return. Pride of ownership is a wonderful thing – if you can afford it.

- Middle of the Roader – not too much work needs to be done. The sellers haven't allowed too much deferred maintenance to pile up, and with a few tweaks here and there, you can make the place look nice, and will be able to raise the rents. Less work, and a constant flow of rental income certainly has a lot to be said for it.

You know how much time and effort you want to put in; you know what kind of property you are looking for, so next you need to consider location. You have three options here:

1. You can choose to purchase your MHP close to home where a simple drive gets you to the front entrance. The downside to this is that there may not be the exact MHP investment that you want just down the road. If being close to your investment is your primary goal, then you may have to change gears on what you are willing to invest in. Prices could be a lot higher where you live so your investment dollars won't go as far as they would if you were willing to travel a bit more.

2. If you can travel a bit - maybe you are willing to drive, or fly, several hours to your MHP. You may find that the park of your dreams is just a six to eight hour trip away. This could make good sense to you if a little travel for a better return is what you are willing to do.

3. Lastly, you may be saying to yourself "I want what I want, and will go where I need to in order to get it." That is how many people, myself included feel. So what if you

have to get on an airplane and fly eight hours and then drive a bit more. If you are getting the monetary returns and the type of investment property that suits your needs, then go for it.

Everyone is different. Only you can decide what is best for you. I have owned parks that took a day of traveling to get to, and a day of traveling to return from. I have owned parks that were almost in my back yard.

If you are a hands-on type and enjoy knowing your manager and tenants on a more intimate level, or you are buying a fixer upper that needs your expertise, or you don't want to do a lot of traveling, you may decide that you want to buy a park in your town.

However, there can be downsides to having a property in the same town you are currently living in. Twenty five years ago, I moved my family from California up to Montana. We wanted a better life for ourselves and our children. Little did we know that Californians moving to Montana were the equivalent to telling the Hatfield's that you are a McCoy.

Montanans are a friendly, open hearted group of people – just don't move to their state and try and "Californicate" it. Montanans have their own traditions and way of doing things – **adapt to it or get out** - seemed to be the motto back in 1991. To be honest, I had to agree with them, after all, "why change a good thing?" However, as you learned from my upscale community building plans, I didn't always know I was trying to change what my neighbors felt "didn't need changing", and found myself in deep doo doo.

Moving to the town where I had purchased and owned four parks meant I was the largest landlord in the area. According to our landlord/tenant attorney I had made myself a big target for anyone, or any group, who had a grievance about anything real or imagined.

It wasn't very long before I found out that small town folks who say they don't want anyone in their business were more than happy to get into mine. Not that I blamed them. The area was just being discovered by famous folks who were busy buying up all available land and homesteads at low prices. Very quickly, land and home prices began to soar. Locals soon found they couldn't afford to live in their own home town anymore.

Anyway, as if my attorney had peered into a crystal ball, it wasn't very long before I was famous. If I was cleaning up a park and requiring the tenants to do the same, it made the newspaper because I was "diminishing the tenant's standard of living".

If I raised the rents, it made the newspaper because I was "taking advantage" of my low income tenants (mostly college students).

If I changed the rules and regulations to match Montana law and guarantee that each tenant was treated the same as their neighbor, I made the newspaper because I was "being unfair." This was a time when a landlord had the right to evict anyone for "no reason at all" and would not be breaking the law!

Like I said, I became famous really fast and sometimes it was embarrassing. One day my wife and I walked into a restaurant and I heard some folks whispering that they had seen me on TV.

I owned those parks for 15 years before moving on to bigger properties, which may I add - were out of state.

That brings me to the upside of having property far away from where you live. In addition to having a nice degree of anonymity, you might also be able to buy a larger, better cash flowing MHP. Being a distance away, you will have to make sure that the on-site management team you hire and train really understands their jobs, and if in doubt won't hesitate to contact you for advice.

 When hiring any employees, it is always best to run background checks, call all references and past employers, and have some serious questions to ask and get good answers to, when you do your face to face interview. A good manager can grow your business; a bad one can sink it. Proper training, a thorough manager's manual, and support from you, will make all of the difference.

Visit your out of the area MHPs on a regular basis and be sure you don't tell your employees when you are coming. It never hurts to know your people are doing a good job all of the time and not just when they know you are coming out to see them.

If this is starting to sound a bit like making your life harder, then a great solution is to hire a property management company that specializes in MHPs. Cost for professional management can run anywhere from 5% to 10% of the gross income.

"Wow," you are probably saying.

"Well worth it," I say. A likely scenario follows:

You are in Hawaii enjoying the fruits of your labors. The entire sewer system in your Arizona Park bursts, creating a health hazard. The management company calls to inform you of the situation, and let you know they are on top of the issue. They make sure that the tenants know the problem is being solved.

You are happy to hear how your management company is taking care of things. Best of all, once you hang up the phone you are free to sigh in relief and have another sip of that Pineapple Martini. Awww, I love getting my tan on.

A good management company can also help you make more money from your property. They have a handle on what other MHP owners are doing by way of rent raises, advertising, or property improvements. A good management company knows the most cost effective methods in which to maintain a park, and where to find the best sub-contractors to get jobs done. Believe me, a good management company is worth every penny you pay them.

Of course, maybe you are like me and will never take a "hands off" approach. I have owned my own management company for the past 30 years. I have never been one to shy away from hard work. If I ask an employee to do some God awful job, then I am willing to do it with them. If ditches are to be dug, I'll always have a shovel in my hands and the dirt will be flying. I want my employees to know that I am just like them and am willing to chip in to get the job accomplished.

I enjoy the property management business almost as much as I enjoy owning properties. The benefit to me in owning properties is that if I ever decide that property management isn't fun anymore, I can always retire and let someone else do the work while I go on a cruise somewhere far away (one of these days I'm going to visit Australia).

Recap On Where to Begin

- What are your investment goals?
- What kind of return on your money do you want to receive?
- What kind of property meets your needs – upper level, lower level, or mid-range level?
- Where will your property be located?

Chapter 8

WHERE TO FIND THE BEST MOBILE HOME PARK FOR YOU

So Many Things to Consider

You have created your investment goals. You have a general idea as to where you want your property to be located. You also know what kind of property condition is just right for you.

"So where the heck can I find my MHP?" you ask.

I often begin my MHP quest with an internet search on LinkedIn (http://www.linkedin.com), Loop Net (http://www.loopnet.com), or just a good old "Google" search, and then the Mobile Home Park Store (http://www.mobilehomeparkstore.com .

After checking out the above sites, I will also go "old school" and make cold calls. Yep, it still works. If you are good with people, enjoy talking to strangers and know what you are looking for, this is a great way to go. You can get lists of mobile home parks in the area you are interested in from a good old fashioned phone book (if you can find one), or online, or sometimes even city hall. The idea is to look at the address locations, and let your fingers do the walking.

If I am in a traveling mood I will drive out to areas I am interested in. I call this "trolling for parks." If I see a park manager, I will stop the car and have a talk with them. I let them know I'm looking to buy a park in the area. I have found **many** parks for sale by going out and meeting with managers.

People love to be helpful, and in helping you get some of your questions answered, they might volunteer that the owner is getting on in years, or a child inherited the property, and are pretty tired of it and might be willing to sell.

You can also ask straight out if the owner might consider selling and see if you can get the owner's name and phone number. Generally, a good manager won't give you this information, but I have had some do it, especially if the present owners are not doing a very good job. If you can't get the owner's number, then ask the manager to take yours and pass it on. If the manager likes you and does not feel that their job is threatened, they will most likely do just that.

A manager who feels you are going to change things in a major way, which *may* include getting rid of them, will be of no help to you. I always ask the manager how long they have been the manager; if they like the job and if I did purchase the park, would they be willing to stay on and work for me. They like the security in that.

I also look on Craig's List, at the free newspapers I find at grocery stores and read *real* print, and on line newspapers.

Another way to scout MHPs for sale is to call banks. There are many viable investments that have been mishandled by the owners and have been repossessed by the bank. There are parks that go on the auction block and you can be the lucky "winner" of one of these bank owned investments.

The best way to find these kinds of properties is to call all of the local banks in the area you are looking in; call some of the major manufactured home community loan brokers.

If you don't feel confident in your abilities to find the right park for you, or are not sure how to make a deal on a property on your own - find a real estate broker who *specializes* in mobile home parks and nothing else. Ask them questions; how long they have been in this particular industry? How many parks have they sold and do they now, or have they ever, owned a manufactured home community? You want someone to help you that really knows the business, not just one who sells it.

Why not hire your friend down the road who sells houses to be your agent? Because they don't know the ins and outs of the business. The MHP industry is highly specialized; it is different from apartments, houses and shopping centers. There are things to look for when buying a park that are particular to this industry alone.

 You will find specialty brokers at:

 Amorgin Investment Group, LLC (http://www.amorgininvestmentgroupllc.com call me, **Dave Rousher**, at: **208-661-9799**) Marcus &Millichap (http://www.marcusmillichap.com) , CBRE (http://www.cbre.com), LinkedIn https://www.linkedin.com and the Mobile Home Park Store http://www.mobilehomeparkstore.com.

Recap – Where to Find the Best Park for You

- Linked-In, Loop Net, The Mobile Home Park Store, Google search

- Telephone book

- Drive through parks and talk to the managers

- Craig's List

- Banks

- Realtor who specializes in MHPs such as Dave Rousher with Amorgin Investment Group, LLC at: http://www.amorgininvestmentgroupllc.com/contact.html **Dave Rousher, 208-661-9799.**

Chapter 9

FOUND THE PARK OF MY DREAMS

What Do I Do Next?

So, you have found the park of your dreams. You are interested in buying as soon as possible. Don't be too hasty! I have more ideas that will help you become completely sure that you are making the best decision with your investment dollars.

To begin with, get a map of the area that the MHP is located in. Look closely at the cities and towns in that area. Eliminate any place that has a population of less than 50,000 people. Small towns may have great atmosphere but you won't have a large pool of tenants to draw from.

Take it from me, I purchased a park an hour out of Billings, Montana, in a cute town near a tourist attraction. I figured it wouldn't be too hard to manage since I lived in the state and it was only three hours from my home.

At the time, the lack of population in the town didn't bother me. The park had a few vacancies I planned on filling up and getting some nice tenants into. Sadly, and very quickly, I learned that the park's tenants were not the kind I normally enjoyed working with. To give you an idea, one of the park rules was that "no one is allowed to be intoxicated outside of their mobile home," and another was that "liquor bottles and beer cans cannot be used as house decorations." I had never heard of rules like those in all of the years I had owned MHPs. I think I was just too stupid to run!

This is the park that taught me to stick with the 50,000 people rule. With a population base of that size, I am sure you will find enough sober tenants to live at your MHP.

Once your city is identified, draw a circle around it. This circle should encompass no more than five miles outside the city limits. The further out of town your park is located, the less population pool you will have to draw from, and the lower the rents on your property are likely to be.

Next, divide your circle into four equal "pie" pieces. You have now cut your city into quadrants for research purposes.

Every city has a good side, a bad side, a better side and a best side. Depending upon the type of investor you are is where you will concentrate your MHP search efforts.

If you don't care what part of town your investment will be located in, then just skip over the next couple of paragraphs. If you do care, then here is where you begin:

Call the Chamber of Commerce and let them know that you are from out of town and are interested in purchasing property in their "wonderful" city. Tell them what you are looking for as far as neighborhood demographics. Ask them if they have any suggestions or ideas as to what might be the best part of town for you to consider.

Go online and look at the local newspaper(s) crime reports. Check your map to ascertain where the most, or least, amount of crime is occurring and what kind it is.

I purchased a park once that was *close* to a good neighborhood area. If I had done my homework more thoroughly I would not have purchased that investment. If I had done my homework I would have learned that burglaries occurred there almost daily, and drug deals and busts were a weekly occurrence.

Just about the time I was selling the property, one of my tenants stabbed her boyfriend 20 times in front of the bus stop just as school children were coming home. A crowd gathered as the woman screamed at the police asking if her boyfriend was dead. She wanted to know because if he wasn't, she'd be glad to make sure he was. Way too scary stuff!

Do your homework. *PLEASE.*

Many times, the police will be happy to give you their input on the different areas of the city.

Another idea is to cold call local businesses and ask whoever answers the phone about the area. I have found that when I am open and honest with my reasons for inquiring, that people are generally more than happy to give me their opinions. One thing to remember however, is that everyone creates their personal opinions from life experiences, one person may hate a particular location while another loves it. Ask around and you will get a general idea.

Go online and Google the statistics on the city you are interested in. Is the unemployment rate higher or lower than the national average? Obviously, the lower the unemployment rates the better.

If the unemployment statistics meet your criteria, then check and see who the current companies offering jobs are. Are they from one company, or many? Are the businesses providing this employment stable – growing – or slowing failing?

If all of the jobs in the area are from a single source I would be wary. What if the company decides to move to another location? Just think about what has happened to Detroit, now that the automotive industry is no longer a strong force there.

I have always made it a practice to NOT invest in an area where the sole reason businesses are surviving is from a military base. Government cuts, or deployments, can quickly kill your tenancy and/or tenant abilities to make rent. This can and does happen, so please do your homework.

University and government towns seem to be pretty stable economically. Universities historically have always had students, which mean tenants for you. As for government agencies - when was the last time you heard of one being closed down and moved away (except for military bases of course), or any of the agencies cutting jobs?

Another thing to contemplate when choosing a location for your new investment is weather. Ma Nature can wreak havoc on the things that man has built. A tornado, hurricane, or massive snow storm can destroy a MHP. And yes, you as the owner may have insurance on your property, but what about your tenants? Most people are sadly underinsured, and if a massive Hurricane Katrina, or Sandy, comes through your town, you could end up with a piece of land full of scraps of abandoned metal.

Next, check out the cost of living in the area. Is it higher or lower than in other places in the state, or the nation? If the cost of living is lower in the city you have chosen you will have lower rents. Lower rents that can't be raised will make it hard for you to enjoy a profit if expenses go up. A low cost of living to me is a big red **STOP** sign.

If the rents five miles down the road are higher but everything around your prospective property is low with no indication that things are going to be better, then it is time to rethink your acquisition. The same goes for properties 25 miles down the road, people won't commute if they don't have to.

I know of a town located 10 miles from an Air Force Base and 45 miles from a large capitol city. The town has been on a downward spiral for 30 years and as military cuts continue, things are only going to get worse. It is sad because I can tell the town was once a jumping place full of life and prosperity, not so anymore.

What is sad about this location is that most of the MHPs in this town have been so poorly managed, have so much deferred maintenance and have such high vacancy factors that even if the properties were given away, I doubt that they could be resurrected.

Of course the town I am speaking of would not meet my property parameters for purchase because the population is far less than 50,000 and derives most of its economy from a military base.

Next on your list is to check the other parks in the area. Are they all full while the one you are considering has vacancies? Or are *all* of the parks experiencing vacancy issues? If all of the parks have problems, you might want to rethink your purchase.

However, if all of the other parks are full and you find your park is the one with the vacancies, you need to ask yourself "why?" Is it management issues? Does the park have tenants who are on the shady side and running the good tenants out? Find out "why," and then ask yourself if you can fix it?

A lot of times if you get to talking to the managers of competing parks you will find that they are more than happy to tell you what is wrong with the property you are considering. They are often willing to tell you about the area in general and the direction they see the community going. If you speak with more than one manager and hear the same story over and over you will most likely begin to see what reality is.

If your prospective purchase meets all of your investment dreams, then it is time to go out and visit the park. During your visit, be sure to check out other parks in the area to see what they look like. Are they in good shape? Are they in bad shape? What are their vacancies? This will give you a great overview when comparing the property in question and its potential - and you just might find another park to purchase!

Recap – Where to Find a Property

- What part of the U.S. do you want to have your property in?
- Consider the weather extremes and how they might affect your business.
- Population of 50,000 or more.
- Circle a city you are interested in – make the circle a five mile radius from the city center.

- Cut the circle into four nice pie shapes.
- Call around to businesses in the area, check the newspapers, internet news, call the police and see what crime is like in the different areas of your pie.
- Check national statistics for unemployment rates – are they higher or lower than the national average?
- What kinds of manufacturing or businesses provide jobs in the area?
- What is the cost of living in the area compared to the national average? Is it higher or lower?

Chapter 10

WHAT TO RUN FROM

Danger! Danger! Will Robinson!

Blinking red warning signs telling you to "get the heck out of town." Loud speakers blaring "time to flee!" Animated robot flapping his arms saying "danger, danger, Will Robinson . . ." You won't see any of these things, but if you keep your eyes and ears open you will know exactly what to run away from when you encounter it.

As I have already stated, do your homework! Stay away from small population bases. Stay away from cities that are declining in population. Stay away from military towns. Decide if tornados, hurricanes, earthquakes and lots of snow are things that will or won't work for you.

More things to steer clear of are MHPs with **large** vacancies, while being priced as if they are full. Really? Why would I want to buy something that isn't full, but pay a price for it as if it were full? I often wonder what the sellers are thinking.

This is called selling blue sky, and you and I don't need it. If you are interested in blue sky then look overhead on a cloudless day and enjoy all you want for free.

By purchasing a blue sky investment, *you* will be the one spending *your* money to bring in homes, set them up, and get them sold so *you* can fill the park. *You* do all the work to make the park worth what *you* paid for it in the first place.

When you purchase your MHP, you want to go into it making money, not flushing it away. This kind of deal has the seller and real estate agent laughing all the way to the bank. So a rule of thumb is to only buy on the existing Net Operating Income today and forget about "Proformas".

Also, you might want to stay away from mismanaged MHPs with lots of deferred maintenance. Ask yourself the question "If the current owner can't turn the place around what makes me think I can?"

Ask yourself, and be brutally honest:

- Do I have the time, money and expertise to turn this around?

- What experience do I have that is better than the current owner?

- Can I create a game plan that will turn a loser into a winner? Or will I be caught in a continuing downward spiral?

I have seen many parks whose new owners thought they could turn a loser into a winner but lacked the needed skill sets. These buyers should have hired an experienced management company. This would have saved them money at the outset and a lot of Excedrin too.

Another flashing danger signal involves the MHPs that are full, but the park owns most of the homes. Unless you are prepared to be overseer of all of those renters, I suggest you steer clear. It takes a special person to run a rental home business.

Or the park is full, and *someone else* owns the rental homes and is renting the spaces from the owner.

Here is a list of questions that must be answered to your satisfaction before you buy a park full of rental homes owned by someone else:

- What guarantee do you have that the home owner/landlord will maintain his/her homes up to your park standards?

- What recourse do you have if your owner/landlord/tenant fails to pay you your space rent?

- What will your owner/landlord do for you that will ensure that their tenants follow park rules and regulations?

- How did this person end up owning so many homes to begin with?

- And what is keeping the landlord/tenant from moving all of his/her homes off of your property if you and he/she don't agree on management styles? To lose half of your customers would be catastrophic.

This happened to me. I purchased a large park that had 205 rental homes. This equaled about half of the park's spaces. One person owned the homes, and that individual did not choose to enforce park rules, or require that the homes owned by him be maintained at Park standards.

He never paid his rent in a timely manner and refused to pay late fees.

Before I purchased this park I had questioned the seller fairly extensively about this owner/landlord situation and was assured that they had never had any issues. I found out after the fact that they never had any issues because he and the landlord were related!

As the situation evolved, I ended up taking out a $1.5 million dollar loan to purchase the 205 MHs from the owner/landlord. Then I discovered that most of the homes were vacant and the ones that weren't vacant were occupied by *real* trailer trash (prostitutes, drug dealers and users and criminals of all kinds). Because the owner/landlord was related to the seller, he had been propping up the rent payments to the park in an effort to make his rental home investment appear real, and stable, so I would buy him out. This story has a less than happy ending.

Don't make the same mistakes I have made over the years. For every reason I tell you to run, don't walk, away from an investment, I can give you a sad but true story of how I, or someone I know has suffered harsh consequences from not heeding this advice.

Admittedly, some of the harder stories ended up with happy endings, but in general they did not. Don't take a chance on losing your investment when you can just as easily invest somewhere else with a steady economy, steady population growth, high tenant ratings etc.

Recap – What to Stay Away From

(1). Stay away from small population bases.

(2). Stay away from cities/towns where the population is on the decline.

(3). Stay away from military towns.

(4). Decide if hurricanes, tornados and tons of snow are something you can deal with.

(5). Stay away from parks that have huge vacancies and are being priced as if they are full.

(6). Pay for what you are actually getting – that is the land, buildings and *filled* spaces - not Proformas!

(7).   If the property has been mismanaged, are you the person who can turn it around?

(8).   Rental homes can be real trouble unless you have the knowledge and experience to manage them.

Chapter 11

HOW TO MAKE MONEY

Think Like Daddy Warbucks

Just like with any other business venture, the first thing you will have to do is get into the mindset that you will have to work. That is life. I'm here to help you work smarter and not harder. Why reinvent the wheel? If you follow my easy steps to success, you will be lucky enough to bypass some of the crazy errors I made when I started out in this business back in the Stone Age.

To begin with as with all real estate investments, the old adage "location, location, location" still holds true. Follow the steps laid out already - check the economy, find out who is providing jobs, etc. This will help you find your investment winner.

Over 25 years ago, I set my sights on a town in a state that wasn't well known. What I did know was that this state and town had an appeal for me like no place I had visited before. I purchased four parks there and completed my portfolio with six more parks within the state. After I cleaned them up and evicted the riff raff, they turned out to be real money makers with plenty of upside potential and curb appeal.

 The town I'm speaking of is now the very popular city of Bozeman and the state in question of course is Montana. Everything was right and ripe for my purchase power in the area. It was, and still is, a beautiful place to live and the population core was very stable. However, at the time Bozeman did not meet the 50,000 population parameter that I suggest. It did have a University population and was a great tourist hot spot.

Plus I wanted to move there, and having my business out the back door held a lot of appeal at the time. So, we sold our house in California and beat feet to the Last Best Place, so we could enjoy the Big Sky Country. The State of Montana was where I invented the wheel, slew dinosaurs and earned my mobile home park owner chops.

However, in the end I knew I had made the right decision. My first park purchase was on the Gallatin River and despite the fact that the park was old, full of druggies and prostitutes, and needed tons of work, I could see that potential was there.

Due to the mismanagement of ownership and disagreements between their partners, I was able to purchase the property for an excellent price. The upgrading process wasn't an easy journey but I was fortunate in that I hired the right management team who helped me turn the place around.

So having told you about my Gallatin River Montana fixer upper, I might as well tell you that I have done very well by purchasing distressed parks. Yep, I said don't do it unless you know you can turn it around.

When I first looked over the rent rolls of that particular park, I knew I could fix what was broken. This was verified the day I personally visited the property and spoke to locals. The problem wasn't the area the park was located in, but the folks who were in charge.

The park manager told me how frustrated he was and what he would do to improve the place if given the opportunity. He knew what he was talking about and had the capability of implementing his plans if given a chance. I could tell that with him on my team we would be able to spin straw into gold.

The first thing we did was clean the place up and evict all of the non-paying tenants. We put in a new set of rules and regulations that were strictly enforced. People who broke the law (yes, I mean the law, not just the rules and regulations) were removed and replaced with new law abiding tenants.

Run down houses were either removed or refurbished by their "new" home owners. Abandoned units were removed and replaced with newer updated homes that buyers stood in line to purchase.

To this day I still have fond memories of living in that park and sitting along the Gallatin River fishing for trout and just breathing in the clean mountain air. I also have memories of becoming instantly famous and notorious because I was changing things in a way that the current tenants didn't want.

When you live in a small town nothing is a secret. Everyone knows your business and what you are doing even before you do.

Twenty Five years later Bozeman is a strong thriving community that is still growing and has plenty of upside potential.

Another way to make money on a new investment is to buy a park that is currently owned by a mom and pop. I did just this in the town of Canon City, Colorado. As with most mom and pops, they lived in the park and knew the tenants (were friends with them). They had not raised the rents in over ten years and hadn't done any real repairs in probably as many years due to their age.

The park was quite run down, but upon close inspection I found that the general bones of the place were good, and what was needed was a good clean-up and some cosmetic repairs. A nice new sign, trees trimmed, streets repaved and get the tenants to clean up their lots and homes. Also, I added an onsite manager who didn't know any of the tenants. The place became a jewel in my portfolio.

Next, if the property you want to purchase has extra land, check with planning and zoning, and see if you can expand your park and add more spaces. I have purchased many a park with a few acres of land that was covered with weeds and garbage that the owners had ignored. After adding more spaces and bringing in new tenants, my cash flow soared.

Mobile home dealers are often interested in bringing homes to parks with new spaces so that they can sell the homes to new clients. Advertising campaigns have also enticed new tenants with nice homes to my properties. If these aren't workable options and you want to bring in homes yourself, be aware that selling mobile homes can be difficult, if not illegal to do because of the Dodd Frank Act – this is something to discuss with your attorney.

If you are not a licensed mobile home dealer you may have to hire someone to originate and service the mobile home loans for you. Selling homes on some kind of payment plan will generate extra short term cash flow and will fill up your park.

Buying homes will add value to your property. An easy example:

Let's say your lot spaces once they are filled, are worth $30,000 and you currently have four vacant spots. By getting homes onto these pads and selling them to paying tenants you will add value to your property. $30,000 for each space X 4 paying homes = $120,000.

For all of you math whizzes out there, don't be insulted by this basic and obviously not real world example. I'm trying to KISS (Keep It Simple Stupid) things here. If you make a profit off each of the homes sold then good for you in generating some short term pocket cash.

If a seller owns homes that are being sold on contract in the park, remember that the income from these homes should not be added to the purchase price. **This income is not permanent**. The only value a mobile home on contract has for a potential park buyer is the value of the home itself and the income it brings in from space rental.

I have seen sellers use the value of the contract homes, the monthly home contract payments, and the space rental income in arriving at a purchase price. A bank won't use anything except space rental income to decide how much a park is worth. Think like a bank and only use space rental when paying for a MHP.

Today there are a few manufactured home manufacturers that will actually help you, the park owner, finance their new homes. One manufacturer requires 15% down and they will finance the balance @8%, principal and interest amortized over 10 years. They will also pay for the transportation and set up.

So, let's take a look at what that would mean. Their average home with transportation and set up is around $40,000. You would put $6,000 down and finance $34,000 at the numbers mentioned above, which would make a monthly payment to you of $412.51. Because you are a nice park owner, you charge your new tenant $45,000 for the same house with $5,000 down payment (I know you paid $6,000 but follow me on this one). You charge them 9% interest with a payment of $506.70 per month. You pocket $94.19 per month for 10 years so you make $5,000 on the price of the home and $11,302.80 over the life of the loan. What is really nice about this is the tenant has a home payment and lot rent of approximately $806.70 which is very affordable and they can have a new home for very little down.

Another idea; if you don't want to put in more spaces, but have that empty area full of weeds and trash that is just begging to add to your bottom line income, is to clean up the mess and fence in the area. You can then charge for RV and extra vehicle storage, which will free up street space, making the park look cleaner while generating extra income.

 If you are able to put in a few storage units, that would also help with the cash flow and increase the property value. People have a lot of "stuff" and if you don't make them keep their lot spaces neat and tidy, that "stuff" will accumulate in and around their mobile homes - guaranteed!

Providing (at a cost of course) storage units will clean up your park and generate some extra income, which also adds to the bottom line value if you choose to sell.

Another way I generate extra money is by looking at what the current owner is spending on expenses. Are there things that could be removed or cut down while still maintaining a rockin' investment? Many parks are not sub-metered for water and sewer. This means that the owner is paying for all of the water and sewer their tenants are using and not passing the expense along to them. Install water meters and begin having the tenants pay for what they use.

In cold states, it is common practice for homeowners to leave a faucet or two running so that their pipes don't freeze. Who is paying for this extra water usage? YOU! Not only is this a waste of our natural resources, it is a drain on your bottom line (pun intended).

A simple thing like heat tape on the pipes going into the house will solve this issue of needing to run water all winter. Let's be honest, why would anyone want to heat tape their water line if *you* are paying the water bills?

By sub-metering, you will have an initial outlay in water meters costs. Those meters will more than pay for themselves when the tenants begin to pay for their own usage. Admittedly, you will still have your own water and sewer bills for your park office or clubhouse, but at least you know it is yours and not someone else's.

Traditionally, space rent included water, sewer and trash. As these expenses went up, park owners learned to pass costs through. Another pass through can be with trash. The old days when the park owner rented a dumpster, or provided for garbage pick-up are over.

Most cities have trash removal down to an art form. They provide the garbage cans and will provide recycle bins as well. Things should be recycled and disposed of in a proper manner. Why should you be the one responsible for and paying for it?

Just like with any community neighborhood, garbage should not be allowed to accumulate at the sides of homes, on front porches or on lawns. The best way for general household garbage to be disposed of is via the city waste disposal system.

Each tenant can sign up for private service as an individual home owner.

If individual garbage service is not available through your city, then find out what is being charged to you for disposal and divide that amount between the spaces and pass the cost on. It will be your manager's job to check what is being put out on garbage day so as to make sure that cans are not overflowing. You will be charged extra for overflow trash. Your manager can make sure that the tenant who incurred the added cost will be charged for it.

If your property is located in a tourist area, like the one I had on the Gallatin River, and if you have extra space out front, why not put in a few RV spaces? RV travel is a popular vacation option and life style now days. Why not cash in on that? You may have to put in showers, a bathroom and a laundry room but you can charge for the shower and laundry usage. This cost will help offset the original cost of putting in the RV section. Shower and laundry charges are great for your bottom line cash intake and property value.

Another way to generate extra income is to charge for pets and guests. Yes, sounds like a petty thing but every penny helps. By charging for pets you can control what breeds, sizes and numbers, your tenants bring in to the park.

Many insurance companies nowadays won't insure you if you allow any of the Bully Breeds on the property. Bully Breeds include Rottweiler's, German Sheppard's, Shar Pei's, Chow Chow's, Doberman's, Bull Terrier's and of course Pit Bull's. I personally don't have anything against any of these breeds. I think it is the owners who have created problem dogs. As a matter of fact I am a long time Rottweiler owner, but I don't live in a MHP where they are an insurance issues.

The reason I charge extra for guests is twofold. The more people living in a home, the more usage is put on the infrastructure of your property. If you have large groups of people living in a dwelling, even if they are paying for the water and sewer, there is still wear and tear on the pipes going in to and out of, the home. These are your responsibility if anything goes wrong with them.

I have always made it a practice to charge for guests after ten days. I charge by the day until they are gone. This will help offset repairs and maintenance in the future and will discourage overcrowding of the mobile homes. I do not allow homes to be overcrowded. A two bedroom home can accommodate four people, not six or eight.

Put in solar panels or wind power generators. Yes, this may sound like a crazy idea but why not use upcoming technology to help pay for electricity? Put solar panels or small wind turbines attached to the office and/or clubhouse to offset costs. Maybe you will be able to put a little extra cash in your pocket by charging the power company for any extra power your generators are making?

You might even try and put solar panels and wind power on that extra piece of land that you don't want to put more pads or storage units on. Sell the power back to the electric company. By getting the OK from the city fathers you can then look for grants that are available to help offset the initial costs.

Lastly, and most importantly, you will make money by raising the rents every year. If you don't do one thing I have suggested above, do not ever *NOT* give out rent raises. Annual rent raises are your bread and butter.

Rent raises keep pace with inflation and also create property value for a future sale. Even if the raise is only $1.00, the tenants get used to the fact that the rents go up.

As I said before, a few tenants will gripe and put up "for sale" signs, but once they get used to the idea that rents will be raised every January (I do this because during the winter it is harder to move and sell a home), they stop complaining because they know it is going to happen and there is nothing that can be done about it.

Cash flow and property value are king in this business. Take advantage.

Recap – How to Make Money

- Get rid of dead beat tenants.
- Rehab or remove vacant homes.
- Bring in new homes and new tenants.

- Buy from a mom and pop.
- Fix deferred maintenance and clean up trash.
- Put in a new sign.
- Put in RV storage and/or storage facilities.
- Put in an RV park section.
- Add laundry and shower area for RV tenants.
- Meter or sub-meter each unit's water and sewer.
- Have tenants pay for their own trash.
- Charge for pets and guests.
- Put in solar panels or wind generators.
- Always give annual rent raises.

I hope you have enjoyed this book. I enjoy helping fellow investors by answering questions and helping them set up MHP purchases. I'm always looking for new investors to partner up in one of the Amorgin Investment Group, LLC MHP projects.

For consultations and questions call David Rousher at: 208-661-9799, or via email at: drousher@gmail.com.

Thank You!

Before you go I would like to thank you for reading my book. There are so many books to read and so much information on line that you can choose from. I am honored that you have chosen *How to Invest in Mobile Home Parks* as your reference guide. Thanks for reading all the way to the end.

 Could I ask you for a small favor? Please take a minute and leave a review for this book on Amazon. This feedback will help me continue to write about my passion of mobile home park investing.

Have any questions about a property you are currently buying, or interested in? How about becoming a partner with Dave Rousher in a profitable MHP Community? Feel free to call me at: **David Rousher 208-661-9799**. Or email me at: drousher@gmail.com. For more info on past projects, check out our website at: **www.AmorginInvestmentGroup.com.**

Many thanks!

Dave Rousher

About the Author

David Rousher has been in the mobile home park business for over 35 years. He has built a valuable reputation in the industry. He is the President of Amorgin Investment Group, LLC (AIG, LLC).

Under Mr. Rousher's supervision, Amorgin specializes in putting investment groups together and purchasing MHPs that are suffering from vacancy problems and deferred maintenance issues.

Prices for these communities are based upon CAP Rates. His experience has created working relationships with brokers, community owners, lenders and manufactured home builders.

Each investment selection is carefully rated and evaluated. At AIG, LLC, Mr. Rousher tries to stay away from large metropolitan areas where investor competition is the greatest. By seeking out parts of the country that are just beginning to experience growth, he has found that greater income and upside potential is available.

AIG, LLC, knows that properties that have been mismanaged and are operating at less than full potential prove to be excellent investments.

Location, price, down payment, financing, cash flow, tax benefits and appreciation potential are all thoroughly considered, as are local market trends and construction quality. AIG, LLC, does everything possible to attain maximum return on investment dollars.

Mr. Rousher is always looking to purchase communities that have a rating of 2 to 3 stars or better, 10 – 30% vacancy factors, and are in a geographical location that is conducive to filling empty spaces with homes to qualified families.

He looks to generate 8-12% cash on cash return at the close of escrow, followed by increases in this cash flow and equity position for himself and his partners.

Contact Mr. Rousher and the Amorgin Investment Group, LLC website at:

http://www.amorgininvestmentgroupllc.com

https://www.linkedin.com/pub/dave-rousher/7/844/65a

Call: 208-661-9799 or email.
drousher@gmail.com